The Path I Didn't Expect

He has shown you, O mortal, what is good.

And what does the Lord require of you?

To act justly and to love mercy

and to walk humbly with your God.

— MICAH 6:8

The Path I Didn't Expect

Orienting My Life in Faithful Service

Allen Pinkley

STEADY CURRENT
PRESS

The Path I Didn't Expect

Orienting My Life in Faithful Service

by Allen Pinkley

Published by

Steady Current Press

Melbourne, Florida

www.steadycurrentpress.com

ISBN 979-8-9950358-0-0 (paperback) | 979-8-9950358-2-4 (ebook) | 979-8-9950358-1-7 (Kindle)

Printed in the United States of America

Proceeds from this work may be directed toward ministries and Scouting programs that embody the values of faith, service, and servant leadership.

Dedication

"Here am I. Send me." — *Isaiah 6:8*

For **Amanda,**
who said "yes" first and kept saying it with me — even when the path was
unclear.

For **Ben**, **Matthew**, and **William,**
each of you have taught me different sides of love, courage, and faith.
You are the living reminders that leadership begins at home and that grace
multiplies through family.

For **every Scout, leader, and friend** who trusted me enough to walk beside
them — you showed me what faithful service truly looks like.

And to the **One who called me,**
thank You for every unexpected turn that led me closer to You.

The path I didn't expect has become the journey I'm most grateful to walk.

Base Camp
(TABLE OF CONTENTS)

Trailhead
(INTRODUCTION)

I didn't plan to be here.

Not here in Florida, or in Scouting, or even in the church I now call home — I mean here, standing in the middle of something that looks suspiciously like God's intent for my life. At least, one way to honor Him with what I've been given: by sharing it with others.

When Amanda first volunteered as a Den Leader, I remember blinking and asking, "You're a *what*?" It wasn't exactly what I expected from the Cub Scout Round Up. I was working odd shifts, and she was home with our three boys. When it finally sank in what she'd signed up to do, I told her I was fully supportive — as long as it didn't interfere too much with family life.

I certainly didn't plan to be involved myself.

But something in me shifted after we relocated, and I started showing up at Scouting events. I began to notice the need — the empty spaces where adults should have been, the boys whose parents dropped them off and drove away.

I wrestled with it for weeks.

Every night before falling asleep, I'd talk with Amanda about it. The feeling wouldn't leave. It sat heavy on my heart.

It wasn't a lightning bolt, just a quiet conviction that settled in:
Maybe it's time to step up.

That quiet yes changed more than I realized. Somewhere in those years, the question of *why* began to take root. It started as a leadership question. I had come across Simon Sinek's TED Talk — Start with Why. The idea hit me hard: great leaders inspire not by what they do, but by *why* they do it.

That thought stayed with me like a compass point I couldn't stop checking. I began asking it of my Scouts:

"Why are we here tonight?"

"Why does this badge matter?"

"Why do you think this skill is important?"

And quietly, I started asking it of myself.

The answers weren't always tidy, but they were honest:
- I'm here because someone needs to be.
- I'm here because others once showed up for me.
- I'm here because serving feels like where I belong.

That *why* brought me back to something I'd forgotten for years — a way of living I first learned as a kid on Jackson Avenue, long before I knew the word *leadership*.

Back then, leadership looked like scraped knees and dirt under my fingernails. It sounded like laughter echoing off garage doors and screen doors slamming at dusk. I spent whole afternoons sketching out how we'd defend our block in our next round of cops and robbers — our own kind of "mission planning," even if we didn't call it that. Jackson Avenue was my first troop, my first congregation, my first lesson in what it meant to care for others — even when nobody was keeping score.

I never planned to tell this story — only to live it. But somewhere between the small yeses and quiet moments of uncertainty, I began to see God's hand guiding more than just my steps.

I still remember the Sunday it all came together — listening as Pastor Ryan shared a message rooted in Scripture yet shaped by the study *Courage: Jesus and the Call to Brave Faith*.

His words challenged us to live boldly for Christ, and in that moment, something stirred deep in me — a quiet sense that my story needed to be told.

It felt less like an idea and more like an assignment — a nudge from God that this story, *my story*, was meant to be shared.

I missed most of the rest of the sermon, scribbling the title of this book and its first outline — themes that had shaped me and experiences that needed to be shared.

If these pages help someone recognize His presence in their own unexpected path, that will be enough.

To God be the glory.

Segment I -

The Quiet Call

Before purpose is spoken aloud, it stirs in the heart. This part reflects on those quiet beginnings — the seasons when faith took shape in small acts of trust and in the lessons that taught when to listen as much as when to lead. These early steps remind us that God's invitations rarely arrive with fanfare; they begin as a whisper that continues to shape us long after we answer.

Chapters within this segment:

Life on Jackson Avenue

I didn't realize it then, but Jackson Avenue was where I first started learning what service looked like in everyday life. It wasn't about rank or recognition, just showing up for the people around you. I think about that sometimes when I drive back through the old neighborhood.

Not too long ago, or maybe longer than it seems, I had the chance to do just that. I felt a little sad at how run-down it looked, nothing like I remembered from my youth. The big tree in the front yard of the house where I grew up was gone. I remembered how I used to struggle just to get up into the perfect sitting spot where I could see the street, and how, over time, I learned to run up, grab the branch, and pull myself into it. Then came the courage to climb higher and see further. Funny how one simple tree could hold so many lessons about growing up.

Truth is, our neighborhood was simple, like a lot of others. Most of the houses looked the same — small, boxy, and a little plain — but that didn't matter much. What I remember most weren't the houses anyway, but the people who lived in them.

There were good people all around who cared about one another. Loretta lived next door, and Phyllis was across the street with her two beautiful, snow-white dogs. I can't remember the name of the older man who lived beside her, but I used to cut his grass when I was a teenager. Another older gentleman lived on the other side of our house; I'm told I used to visit him a lot when I was younger, maybe to hide from chores at home. Over the years, people came and went. New families moved in, kids grew up, and somehow I became the "big brother" on the street.

One of my favorite things to do was walk Phyllis's dogs. At the time, I didn't think about why I was doing it — I just knew I enjoyed it. I'd knock on her door and ask if I could take them out, and she almost always said yes. Sasha and her companion loved to run, so after walking them down the street, I'd let them sprint all the way home. Running the dogs was fun, and I looked forward to it. Only later did I realize that Phyllis was legally blind and couldn't walk them herself. What felt like play to me was quietly helping someone else.

Another short memory that stands out is how my mom worked to give me a sense of independence early on. Cascade Elementary was only a few blocks away, so she let me walk to school by myself — or at least that's what I thought. What I didn't know was that she'd quietly follow behind me, watching until I turned the corner. I think she trusted me; it was everyone else she was cautious about. I'm sure, before that, she'd walked with me a few times, showing me how to stop at each intersection, look both ways, and listen before crossing. At the time, I thought I was learning how to get to school. Looking back, I think she was teaching me how to move through life — pay attention, take care, and know you're being looked after, even when you don't see it.

Not long after, my mom found herself helping with my Cub Scout den. I don't know if she ever planned to be a leader, but someone needed to step up, and she did. She organized meetings, helped us earn badges, and somehow kept us focused when we'd rather be goofing off. I didn't see it then, but she wasn't just helping me. She was showing what leadership really looks like: steady, patient, and done because it's needed, not because anyone's watching.

Looking back, I think a lot of what I learned on Jackson Avenue came from people like her — folks who just did what needed to be done and didn't make a big deal out of it. That quiet example stayed with me. Later, I'd start to see that same spirit show up in other places — at church, in Scouts, anywhere people served because they cared.

Youth Group Memories

> *"Then I heard the voice of the Lord saying, 'Whom shall I send? And who will go for us?' And I said, 'Here am I. Send me!'"* — *Isaiah 6:8*

Life on Jackson Avenue had its own pace — school, church, neighborhood friends, the same few blocks that felt like the whole world. I knew where I fit, at least most of the time. But as I got older, things started to shift. My sister was growing up, my parents were juggling more, and I was asked to reduce my activities.

I'd earned my Arrow of Light and crossed that bridge ready for the next step, but I never made it to a Boy Scout Troop meeting. I'd made a choice — one that came from somewhere deeper than logic, more like a pull of the heart. That pull led me to the youth group. It was different, but familiar in a way — a place to serve, to laugh, to belong. Looking back, it wasn't just a schedule change; it was the next step in who I was becoming.

I didn't always fit in at school. Some of that came down to simple things like clothes or what was considered "cool." But at church, it was different. It was the one place where those things didn't seem to matter. Someone always made sure I could be part of what was happening — a trip, a retreat, a fundraiser. I might not have realized it then, but looking back, I can see there was grace behind the scenes.

That's where Tim Henson comes in. He's been my friend for as long as either of us can remember. We've tried to figure out when it started — maybe the church preschool — but honestly, we were just always there. Tim's the kind of person who sees people. He'd notice when someone was sitting alone or needed a hello.

He never worried much about himself, just about others. We didn't talk a lot about life's heavy stuff; we just enjoyed what was in front of us. There was comfort in that.

Our youth group had its share of fun and chaos. The plays we put on around Christmas, the retreats at Lakeside, the canoe trip where the borrowed Scout tents came loose, and one found its way into the fire pit — all part of growing up. Later, David Knarr joined us, and the three of us became a pretty tight group. Looking back as an adult leader now, I can only imagine the adults' conversations: "What are they going to do next?"

The best stories rarely come from when everything goes right. The chapel window that shattered because someone snuck in from the loft. The pepper spray incident (thankfully, no one was in the bathroom). Those stories are funny now, but what sticks isn't the mischief — it's how our adult leaders handled it. They stayed calm. They talked to us, not at us. They helped us fix what we broke and make it right. They cared about our safety, yes, but also about who we were becoming. They modeled what Christian leadership looks like — patient, consistent, and full of grace.

Among those who shaped us most was Reverend Francie Dailey. She taught our confirmation class and hosted the youth group Super Bowl parties at her home, but her impact went much deeper. Francie insisted that the youth not be hidden away in the basement or the "youth room." She believed we were part of the church now, not someday. She helped form a youth group committee with officers — president, vice president, secretary — and she encouraged each of us to join a church committee and report back. We weren't just a program; we were a part of the body.

Francie's leadership was balanced by others — Tammy Webb, who oversaw education and kept everything running smoothly, and later Joey and Jennifer, young adult leaders who brought energy and connection. They were close enough in age to relate to us but mature enough to guide us. They made faith feel real, not distant. Early on, it was Francie, Tammy, and the parents; later, it was Joey and Jennifer leading from within. It was a gradual hand off — and we didn't realize it at the time, but they were teaching us responsibility through trust.

They cared deeply about us — not as projects, but as people. They made faith feel personal. When I look back, I can see that what they modeled was the same thing I try to pass on to my Scouts now: youth are people, and people matter. Everyone wants to be seen and trusted. When you give someone ownership, you're really saying, "I believe in you." And when people feel trusted and valued, they'll do more than you thought possible — not because they have to, but because they want to.

Some moments from those years still stand out vividly. There was a retreat with the theme "God Doesn't Make Junk." We were given journals and time to think. I remember a poster of a tree with young people at different spots — hiding, climbing, reaching — and the question: Where do you see yourself? I didn't know then that the front-yard tree from Jackson Avenue would come back into my story years later, but it makes sense now. Growth happens in seasons, and sometimes you're behind the trunk, just waiting for the courage to climb.

The "God Doesn't Make Junk" retreat taught me reflection. The mission trip to Steubenville, Ohio, taught me service. We stayed in dorms, ate too much Taco Bell, and painted porches in an old coal-mining town. We handed out food boxes and cleaned walls. I couldn't tell you what we did on which day, but I can tell you that was the first time faith felt like sweat and sore muscles — like doing something that mattered, even if no one was watching.

And then there was Youth Go Global. That was my chance to represent the missions committee and travel to Indiana to meet youth from all over the world. It was the first time I really felt the weight of stepping into something bigger than myself. I was nervous — anxious, even — but excited too. It was an adventure mixed with uncertainty.

When I returned home, I was asked to share about the experience at church. Standing at the pulpit, I gripped the sides to steady myself. I had a script, I got through it, and I survived.

That chapel holds a lot of my story. It's where the window broke, where I first spoke from the pulpit, and where I spent time contemplating big decisions. It's been a place of mistakes, milestones, and commitments. It's funny how God weaves meaning into the places we least expect.

If I could stand in that chapel today and see that younger version of myself—the kid gripping the pulpit, nervous and unsure — I think I'd just smile. He didn't need advice; he needed to know he'd be okay. Every step forward, every moment of uncertainty, would eventually make sense. Faith has a way of doing that — revealing its purpose later, one small piece at a time.

That's what I carry into Scout Sunday this year — the reminder that the youth I'm speaking to are me then. I don't have to be polished. I just have to be real.

During those years, I also got to know Pastor Bill — a retired minister who helped with our missions committee. He carried a quiet wisdom about him. He wasn't loud or demanding, but when he spoke, you listened. He had a way of connecting Scripture to real life — reminding us that faith was meant to be lived, not stored up for Sunday mornings. I didn't know it then, but his calm presence would return in a meaningful way later in my story.

When I left the youth group and graduated from high school, it felt like a clean close to a season. Senior Sunday was strange — everyone had these big plans for college and careers. I didn't have that. What I had was a pull, a gut feeling to enlist. I didn't know how it would go, but I felt like it was where I needed to be. Maybe my faith then was no bigger than a mustard seed, but it was enough to move me forward.

The weeks before leaving were quiet. I resigned from the few jobs I had and spent time walking, thinking, and preparing. My recruiter told me, "Don't turn down the opportunity for training. It may mean more work, but the skills will stay with you." That advice stuck—it was about more than military training; it was about taking on challenges that would shape me.

I think about humility and conviction often, maybe not always in those terms. Humility has always come naturally, though I can't say exactly where it started —maybe my parents, grandparents, or the people at church. As for following my gut, that came from my dad. He once told me about how he wanted to get into computers back when Jobs and Gates were just getting started, but people talked him out of it. He regretted not following his instincts. He told me, "If you feel strongly about something, do it. Don't let others talk you out of it. Even if it's the wrong thing, at least you won't wonder what if."

Between my dad's advice, the lessons from Francie and the others, and everything I learned from youth group, that's where I found my footing in faith — trusting the pull, moving forward, and showing up even when I didn't have the full picture.

Every Christmas Eve, when the lights dim and one candle lights another, I can't help but think back to those years. The glow starts small — a single flame — and then it spreads across the sanctuary until the whole room shines. That's how faith feels to me now. I was never the first light — that belongs to Christ — but I've carried it, passed it on, and watched it reach further than I could ever see. That quiet glow in the faces around me reminds me that the light was never mine to keep. It was always meant to be shared.

Called to Serve

When I left for basic training, it felt like a step I couldn't undo. At Military Entrance Processing Station (MEPS) we took our final oath, boarded the rapid transit in downtown Cleveland, and headed toward the airport. My parents and grandparents waited at the USO — nervous smiles, proud eyes, the kind of moment you don't realize is heavy until you're already walking away from it. Mom hugged me tight. She always tried to hold strength in her voice, but I could feel the emotion underneath. Then it was time to go. The excitement carried me forward, but something in my gut knew things were changing for good.

When the plane landed in Texas that night, the door opened and the humidity hit like a wall. We moved off the plane with purpose, herded into blue school-bus-looking shuttles and told to hurry up and wait. The yelling started quickly — chaos by design. They had to break us down before they could build us up. Sometime around three a.m. we were shown our bunks in the open bay. It was finally quiet, but I don't think I slept. Two hours later the lights snapped on and the shouting started again. By the time my head hit the pillow that next night, exhaustion had become a new language.

A week or so in, things began to settle. Uniforms were issued, routines took shape, everyone learning when to move and when to stand still. That's when my first real lesson in stepping forward showed up — by accident. Our chow-runner, Airman Sheraton, struggled with a stutter that worsened under pressure. Reporting the flight in front of the "snake pit" was brutal for him. One day our TI came storming out of the dining hall, frustration written all over his face.

"Who thinks they can do a better job than Airman Sheraton?"

Before I knew what happened, my right arm shot straight up. What are you doing? I remember thinking. But I cashed the check my hand wrote. The first time I stood in front of those instructors — heart pounding, voice steady — I just focused on doing what I said I could. When it was over, there was only a small nod, but it was enough. I'd learned something that would stick: confidence doesn't wait until you feel ready.

When Sundays came during basic, they felt like a pause — a brief reset. Everyone suddenly became religious — not out of ritual, but out of need. The nondenominational service overflowed with singing and messages of hope, perseverance, and readiness — words perfectly suited for tired hearts and shaved heads. I don't remember every sermon, but I remember the feeling: a few quiet minutes to reset, to remember who we were beneath the uniforms. For that hour, it wasn't about ranks or rules — just people reaching for something steady.

Graduation came soon after. My parents came down, and we spent the day walking the River Walk, seeing the Alamo, catching up. Mom told me later she'd worried after a letter I sent early on, full of doubt, but now she could see I'd grown. When we said goodbye again and I walked back alone toward the dorms, there was a quiet sadness in me. Not weakness — more a realization that home would never feel quite the same. The future was no longer unknown, but it wasn't the same road I'd left behind either.

Tech school at Keesler AFB felt like a slow release back to normal life. The yelling eased, replaced by purpose. We were learning — basic electronics first, then radar theory. My earlier time in vocational school paid off; circuits and systems made sense to me. I started to find joy in understanding how things worked instead of just following orders. I wasn't sought out for leadership there, but I wanted to serve my peers. After a couple of denials, Staff Sergeant Darnes finally gave me a shot as a student leader. Maybe I wore her down, maybe she saw something — either way, it was another step. Marching formations, mentoring new arrivals, even overseeing the weekend "weeds and seeds" crew. It taught me that leadership isn't given by rank; it's earned by presence.

Somewhere in that season, Amanda appeared — completely by accident. I was heading back from the Vandenberg Center, the little hangout we called "The V," and she was walking the other way. I joked that nothing was happening there, and somehow we ended up sitting in the courtyard sharing a cheap pizza from one of the Domino's drivers who always brought extras. I'd told myself I'd be single forever, but something about her was different — warm, steady, real. We spent evenings talking until curfew, weekends together when we could sign out. I even called my dad and said, "Something's different about her." He'd always told me to trust my gut. He was right again.

In just two months and three days, we were married — in the same church chapel where I'd once sat during youth group, now standing at the front with Pastor Bill officiating. When I called to ask if he would perform the service, he half-jokingly asked, "You in trouble?" I laughed and told him no — this was about faith, not consequence.

The ceremony was small but full of warmth. Tim stood beside me as best man; at the reception he managed to get cake on me, and I chased him into the icy parking lot — blues, dress shoes, and all. It wasn't a grand wedding, but it was ours. Amanda was steady, supportive, and strong-willed enough to keep me grounded.

Those months were full of learning — technical, personal, relational. I was discovering that understanding systems and understanding people weren't all that different. Both required patience, observation, and care. The whisper of calling that had followed me since I left home grew clearer in those days. Service wasn't just about uniforms or duty; it was about trust. You're not above or below anyone. You learn to rely on each other, to carry one another when it counts. You become family — brothers and sisters who don't always get along, but who stand together when things get tight.

I'd learned to say yes, to step forward and serve. What I hadn't learned yet was how to wait — how to listen when the next step wasn't clear. The lessons ahead wouldn't come from training manuals or rank; they'd come from the space between orders and obedience. I didn't know it then, but saying yes was only the beginning. The real test of faith would come in learning when to pause, trust, and move only when the still voice said, "Now."

Between Orders and Obedience

Leaving tech school and arriving at my first duty station, I thought I knew what service meant. I'd learned to follow orders, keep my bearing, and finish the task. But what came next would test something deeper — the space between discipline and discernment, between following commands and learning when to trust the quiet nudge inside. Those years would teach me that obedience wasn't just about rules. It was about responsibility, trust, compassion, and faith.

Billy Turk reminded me a little of my Grandpa Anderson — knowledgeable, sharp, and just ornery enough to keep you guessing. You never quite knew where the line was with him, and that made me cautious. I'd come out of tech school confident, ready to prove myself, but Billy had a way of stripping that polish off quick.

He was the main qualifier for our shop at Tyndall AFB. The rest of the crew handled most of the day-to-day training, but when it came time to certify, Billy was the one standing there, arms crossed, watching every move. He'd ask direct questions, expect correct answers, and keep watching until you either got it right or tripped over yourself. At the time, it felt like he enjoyed making us nervous. What I didn't see yet was that he was testing more than knowledge — he was testing composure.

The part that used to drive me crazy was his insistence on the Technical Orders. Even when I knew the answer, he'd say, "Show me where it says that." I'd roll my eyes, flip through the manual, and point to the same thing I could have said from memory. I went home more than a few nights grumbling about him, venting to Amanda about how impossible he was. What I didn't realize then was that every time I searched for an answer I already knew, I was learning a dozen more I didn't.

It wasn't until years later, while working radar evaluations at Hill AFB with the RADES, that it clicked. I was in a debate with another technician over a system fault, and before I even thought about it, I swung open a TO, flipped to the right page, and pointed. No hesitation. The argument ended, but the light bulb turned on. Billy Turk hadn't been testing my patience — he'd been building my foundation. He taught me that there's a process and a reason for it. In our line of work, mistakes didn't just ruin someone's day — they could cost lives. Obedience wasn't about doing what you were told; it was about honoring the process that kept people safe.

I didn't thank him then, but I carry his lesson still. The next test of responsibility wasn't on the radar, though — it came late one night, just after a training class, when Amanda told me her water had broken.

It must have been close to midnight when I walked through the door after that radar class. I'd been running on fumes and was already halfway to bed when Amanda said her water had broken. For a second, my brain didn't catch up with my ears. One minute I was thinking about system diagnostics and night-shift schedules, the next I was standing in the living room wide awake, adrenaline kicking in where caffeine couldn't.

I must have changed clothes in record time. Whatever fatigue I'd been carrying was gone. The Air Force had trained me to stay calm under pressure, but nothing in the manuals prepared me for this.

We got to the hospital, and from there it all blurred together — the monitors, the bright lights, the nurses coming and going. The videos they made us watch never came close to the real thing. Watching Amanda push through wave after wave of pain, I realized how little control I actually had. She was fighting through something raw and powerful, and I could only hold her hand and try to steady her breathing when mine wanted to race.

And then suddenly, it was over. The room that had been filled with tension went quiet except for a single new cry. A nurse handed me the smallest human I had ever seen, and every thought about what I had to do next disappeared. All the training, all the procedure, all the plans — gone. What was left was simple and final: you are a parent now.

There's no briefing or checklist for that moment. It's not about being ready; it's about realizing that ready or not, you are now responsible. This little life depended on me. And just like that, service took on a new definition. The responsibility I'd been learning in uniform became something entirely different — something closer to love.

When I arrived at Tyndall fresh out of tech school, MSgt Woody Crist was already the shop supervisor — the kind of leader who set the tone the moment he walked in. He wasn't above getting his hands dirty and never asked anyone to do something he wouldn't do himself. He had that quiet, steady authority that made you want to do things right, not because you were told to, but because you didn't want to let him down.

That day was routine. We were both outside cutting grass around the radar site — Woody riding the mower and me following behind with the push mower. The Florida heat was thick, the kind that stuck to your sleeves and made even the simplest work feel slow. We'd settled into that easy pattern of shared labor when the call came through: the radar was down.

Woody throttled down the rider just enough to look over and say, "You've got this," before circling the mower back into its path. That was it. No questions, no checklist — just confidence.

I stayed calm until I stepped into the shelter. The familiar cold hit me, the steady hum of the transmitters filling the air. I took a deep breath and exhaled slowly. He believes you've got this — so get it. I started checking readings, and within minutes isolated the issue. It only needed a small tweak, but enough to remind me that little things matter when big systems depend on them.

When I stepped back outside, the radar functioning again, Woody didn't say a word. He just kept mowing, the same steady circles, as if nothing had happened. But that was the point — there was nothing more to say. He already knew.

It took me a while to realize what that moment meant. Woody had been watching since the day I arrived, quietly gauging what I could handle. That day, he gave me more than a task; he gave me his trust. Through his confidence, I learned to find my own. Sometimes leadership isn't about standing over someone's shoulder — it's about standing back and letting them rise.

Hill Air Force Base was different from anywhere I'd been before. The Radar Evaluation Squadron — RADES — didn't maintain a single radar system. We traveled to evaluate others. Every time we arrived at a site, we were treated as the subject-matter experts, even if I'd never seen that particular radar before. It was a strange kind of confidence to grow into — equal parts excitement and quiet pressure. Looking back, it was also my first step toward the aerostat radar systems I'd later work on in the Keys.

What I remember most about Hill wasn't the equipment; it was the people. Our Wing Commander had a way of making everyone feel known. The first time he visited, I was walking down the hall when he stopped me and asked, "How are you and Amanda settling in here?" I was stunned. He barely came to Hill twice a year, yet he knew who I was, and even that we'd just moved in. I later learned that before each visit, he studied photos and bios of every airman and their families. It wasn't for show — he genuinely cared. He wanted us to know that we mattered beyond the uniform.

That same spirit carried through when Ben and Matthew were born. They arrived seven weeks early and spent as many weeks in the NICU. My leadership told me to check in every other day, let them know how the boys and Amanda were doing, and focus on my family. They'd reach out if they needed me. It wasn't just permission — it was support. We had an unwritten rule: self, family, unit. If you or your family weren't okay, you couldn't give your best to the mission. And for once, that wasn't just something we said — it was something we lived.

Looking back, I see how surrounded I was by mentors, even though I didn't call them that at the time. I just felt seen and cared for — part of a greater family. In turn, I wanted to do my best to live up to what I'd been given. Those lessons in grace and compassion left a deeper mark than any technical training. Service wasn't just about readiness anymore. It was about belonging, empathy, and being trusted to care for others as you'd been cared for.

Travis Air Force Base felt almost familiar when we arrived. Amanda and I had visited California once before while stationed at Hill, and the landscape already carried a quiet pull. Funny enough, I'd met someone from RADES while at Tyndall, and even visited the radar site in Cudjoe back then — little strings connecting what I couldn't yet see. Now I was a Staff Sergeant, seasoned and confident, ready for the chance to take on more responsibility. I thought I knew what service was.

Then came the injury. It happened during intramural soccer when an opposing player and I both went to kick the ball at the same time. The impact knocked me down, and I came down hard on my knee. I tried to keep playing, but it didn't last long.

What followed wasn't dramatic — just grinding. Physical therapy, limited workouts, weight creeping up, morale sliding down. I'd been on and off the fitness program before, but this time it hit harder. Each ninety-day waiver felt like a ticking clock. On the ninety-first day, the captain would be at my door, reminding me it was time to get back out there. I'd try, end up back at medical, and start the cycle again. When I asked why I couldn't just get a longer waiver, they told me it was to avoid triggering a medical review board.

It eventually healed, but by then I was behind. And then, one morning, my name appeared on the list. The Air Force was downsizing. I was being cut loose.

Panic hit first — wife, kids, bills to pay, what now? I went to the base chaplain in desperation. I don't remember much of what we talked about. I remember leaving and heading back when a calm came over me — a peace I couldn't explain. Then the thought came: You're an electronic technician, not someone who just hands out basketballs. You can find something. And with that came direction.

When it came time for my final fitness test, I did every sit-up but one. I intentionally stopped just short of passing. It wasn't failure; it was faith. My quality of life had been unraveling for months, my body worn down, my spirit restless. I'd tracked every workout, every meal, every weigh-in, trying to make the numbers make sense. One month the weight went down and the tape went up; the next it flipped. No one could explain it, and I couldn't keep living that way. So I made a choice. This time, my release would be on my terms — an act of trust, not surrender.

Within days I saw a listing for a job in the Keys. Within three, I had an offer.

When I think back on it now, it wasn't rebellion. It was obedience of another kind — the quiet faith that stepping away was part of the call to serve in a new way. The uniform was ending, but the mission wasn't.

From Billy Turk's lessons in humility to Woody Crist's quiet trust, from the chaos of William's birth to the grace shown at RADES and the faith that led me out of Travis, each step taught me something new about obedience. At first, it looked like following orders. Then it became accepting responsibility. Later, it grew into trusting others, showing compassion, and finally, having the courage to let go.

Service had changed shape, but not purpose. The same call that once said "Follow" was now saying "Go."

 TRAIL MARKER I -

Foundations of Service

Every journey begins quietly — in the places where character is formed long before calling is understood. The lessons of childhood, the belonging of youth group, and the first small yeses of service became the groundwork for everything that followed.

I once thought obedience was mostly about action — about saying yes and moving forward. But those early years taught me that sometimes obedience is about stillness: about listening, waiting, and trusting that God's direction often comes between the orders and the understanding.

Those moments never felt extraordinary, yet they shaped how I would serve. The foundation was set, even when I couldn't see where the path would lead.

"When the time is right, I, the Lord, will make it happen." — Isaiah 60:22

Reflective Questions

1. What ordinary moments in your early life taught you quiet lessons that still guide you today?
2. When have you learned that obedience can mean waiting rather than acting?
3. Who showed you that service can be simple — done because it's needed, not because it's noticed?
4. How might God be preparing you now in ways that are easy to overlook?

Closing Prayer

Lord, thank You for the quiet beginnings — for the people and places that shaped me long before I understood Your purpose.

Teach me to notice Your presence in small, ordinary moments.

When I'm tempted to rush ahead, remind me that stillness can be obedience too.

Strengthen the foundations You've laid in me so that every "yes" I offer honors You

Amen.

The path of service becomes real when faith meets opportunity. Scouting offered both — a place to lead, to stumble, and to grow. Each challenge refined what it meant to serve with humility and strength, to trust others, and to find joy in guiding rather than directing. In this stretch of the journey, leadership was learned the long way — by walking beside instead of ahead.

Chapters within this segment:

The First Yes

It wasn't an invitation that pulled me in. No one asked, I wasn't cornered at a meeting, and no guilt-ridden speech sealed my fate. It was an observation — the kind that comes quietly, that silent realization about what will happen if no one does something. The Cubmaster and Assistant Cubmaster both had sons only in Webelos, which meant the clock was ticking. When their boys would cross over, so would they. At most, we had two years before the pack would be without either a Cubmaster or the assistant.

I could already imagine that future meeting — the uncomfortable silence, the awkward pause before someone says, "We need someone to step up." I didn't want to be part of that silence. Amanda was already helping with William's den, and Ben and Matthew would soon be old enough to join — they were already tagging along as 'Scout Buddies'. We were still new to the area but weren't going anywhere soon. After a few weeks of quiet reflection and late-night talks before bed, we agreed I'd step up. I offered a solution before the problem was announced: I'd serve as Assistant Cubmaster now and, when the time came, move into the Cubmaster role.

At first, it was simple enough — learning the books, the verbiage, and the structure of meetings. It was about understanding how things worked, how people worked. But somewhere along the way, that sense of duty began to stretch into something else. I remember telling my boys, maybe half-serious, that even if they decided they didn't want to Scout anymore, I'd still be here. Maybe I didn't realize it then, but that was the moment I started to belong — not just as a parent, but as part of something larger.

Looking back, I think God was already nudging me — not with a dramatic call, but with a gift of observation. He gave me eyes to see a need not yet spoken, and the willingness to act before I felt ready. Life began to widen from work, home, and our small family into something bigger — a kind of extended family I didn't know I needed yet.

Award nights always made me sentimental. Watching those boys — not just mine — come up to the campfire when called to get their recognition, a little taller each time, a little more sure of themselves, stirred something in me. It wasn't one big realization but a slow drip of purpose. Each salute, each grin, each handshake was a reminder: this mattered. And it all started with one small, quiet yes.

Serving the Bigger Picture

It started back in the Cub days — before I ever imagined being part of anything beyond a pack meeting. We were at roundtable when the question went out for someone to chair the next District Cuboree. The room was quiet just long enough for me to open my mouth and say, "Sure, I guess I can do it."

I didn't know what I was signing up for, but I knew I could plan. My schedule for that weekend was tight, every activity stacked like pieces in a game of Tetris. I thought that's what good leadership looked like — cover every minute, anticipate every problem, make it all fit.

Then the morning came. Our District Director, Matt Vercher, showed up smiling and introduced a few extra guests he had "forgotten" to tell me about — the bird lady who rescued injured wildlife and a nearby animal hospital crew. They had no set time limit, no place within my schedule. Everything I'd outlined came unraveled.

I must have looked ready to burst, because Matt pulled me aside and asked, "What do you see?"

At first I didn't get it. I rattled off what was wrong, what was off schedule, what was slipping. He waited. Then I looked around — the Scouts laughing, wide-eyed at the hawks and owls, leaders chatting instead of hurrying them along — and I said, "They're having fun."

He nodded. "Exactly."

That was the day I stopped trying to fill time and started trying to fill purpose. Quality over quantity. Plan, yes — but leave room for discovery and flexibility.

I volunteered again for the next event, this time sharing pieces of the work instead of clutching it all. That second "yes" drew me deeper into district service, where I eventually became the Camping and Activities Chair. It also opened my eyes to what leadership looked like when it wasn't about control.

Matt stayed close through those years — mentor, friend, almost family. He once shared Follow Me Boys with me, saying it captured what this was really about. He and his wife shared a birthday with Ben and Matthew. Before long, he felt like an uncle in every way that mattered. His calm, his humor, his sense of people — all of it modeled a kind of steady grace I wanted to learn.

Then there was Gary McKee, our troop chaplain, who carried quiet faith in everything he did. Well into his later years, he still showed up, still served, still gave more than many who had far fewer limitations. His favorite line—"I wish I could do more"—wasn't self-pity. It was gratitude disguised as humility. He reminded me that serving others is the truest reflection of living like Christ.

Larry Hribar brought history, tradition, and just enough mischief to say, "Let's do it anyway" when an idea didn't fit the mold. Herb Bradshaw, a fellow Buckeye, understood that Scouting wasn't about knots and tents — it was about building character. Together we challenged the norms, always asking how an event could speak to something deeper than logistics.

Those friendships were the easy part. The draining part came from the few who seemed determined to stall progress, often without offering another way forward. For a while I endured it quietly. Then I attended Wood Badge and learned about the stages of change. That perspective shifted everything. Instead of trying to convince everyone, I looked for the willing and moved ahead with them. Resistance didn't vanish, but vision carried more weight when it was shared.

Through it all, I kept seeing how things somehow worked out — never perfectly, but right enough. It wasn't luck. It was teamwork and timing, the right people in the right place, each moved by something placed in their heart. I didn't call it faith then, but I see it that way now.

Looking back, the Cuboree wasn't just a weekend event. It was a small nudge from God: slow down. Be present. This journey isn't about racing to awards or positions; it's about growing together, youth and adults alike, right where you stand.

Matt, Gary, Larry, and Herb all left their fingerprints on me, and through me, on others. I've tried to carry pieces of each of them while staying true to who I am. Their influence didn't change my personality — it deepened my authenticity.

When obstacles came later, what kept me going wasn't pride or stubbornness — it was the people who saw the same horizon. We believed in the impact we could make together for the youth entrusted to us.

That's what serving the bigger picture came to mean: to live a life of service and sacrifice that speaks louder than words, to follow Christ's path without always announcing it. My sons saw it in action, not in sermons — the quiet persistence of a servant leader, trying to walk faithfully, one step at a time.

The Course that Changed Everything

When I first signed up for Wood Badge, I was still finding my footing as a Cubmaster. I didn't just want to run a pack — I wanted to understand it. The purpose, the structure, the "why" behind the methods and structure of the program — even how those lessons would later carry into the troop level, helping me prepare my Scouts more intentionally. I knew that knowledge gives confidence, and confidence builds trust. We'd had some push back within the pack, and I remembered Billy Turk's lesson that knowledge and facts are the foundation for strong, respectful arguments. So, I wanted that foundation — to know where the black and white ended, and the gray began.

It wasn't an easy choice. The course cost more than I could comfortably afford at the time, but through council assistance — and I believe a helping hand from a Scouter in the Keys — I found a way to go. Looking back, that's fitting. Service has always been about others giving of themselves to make something possible for someone else. This was no different.

In our district back then, attending Wood Badge was rare. At the time, I may have been the only active volunteer who had completed the course — and even looking back now, more than a decade later, that number has never been large. There wasn't much local guidance to prepare me, and maybe that was a gift. When I arrived, everything felt new — the sorting into patrols, the staff filling every leadership role, the structure that placed us in the shoes of new Scouts. It wasn't just classroom learning; we were living the Scouting experience again, discovering how it felt to stand on the other side of the program we led. For those few days, we were the Scouts — and that shift alone taught me more than any syllabus could.

One of the earliest moments that stuck with me was a game called "Win All U Can." It came right after another competitive challenge, so the energy was high, and everyone was eager to win. Each patrol had a sign — beads on one side, ax and log on the other. On a count, we had to choose a side, and the combinations determined who gained or lost points. At first, it seemed simple. But as the rounds went on, it became clear that every "win" came at someone else's expense. There was even an option where everyone could earn a few points — far less than the big risks, but enough if we'd chosen to cooperate. We didn't. During the out-brief, one participant grew visibly upset — embarrassed by their choices, realizing they had focused on winning for themselves and their patrol, and had missed the larger purpose. That hit me.

It was a game about integrity, cooperation, and perspective — about asking, "At what cost?" Sometimes you can win the fight and lose the war. Sometimes "winning" isn't the point at all.

Another exercise used a simple water rocket. The instructions were incomplete, the materials inconsistent. Frustrating, but intentional. We were being reminded that Scouts often experience the same thing — unclear directions, missing pieces, expectations without explanation. Our patrol managed to get ours off the ground, though I can't remember how high. What mattered was that we kept working together, doing our best with what we had. In that way, the Cub Scout motto — Do Your Best — fit perfectly. We weren't expected to achieve perfection, just to give our full effort, to bring what we could and trust the rest to the team. Leadership is like that — rarely clean, rarely complete, but always collaborative.

When I returned from the course, something had changed — not in a single flash, but in the quiet way confidence settles in after growth. I understood the "why" more clearly, and I found myself communicating with purpose. I even developed an outline for new parents, a sort of onboarding guide for the pack, and wrote my own vision statement for where we were heading. It was clarity born from understanding, and understanding born from experience.

My Wood Badge Ticket reflected where I was at that moment in my Scouting journey. I wanted to bridge the gap between our pack and the church that chartered us — to make sure we weren't just guests in their hall but partners in purpose. I set goals to improve communication, mounted a bulletin board in the fellowship hall to share updates, and personally invited the pastor and congregation members to our events. For a while, that bridge held. We saw the pastor join us for derbies and ceremonies, and though the relationship later faded, it mattered that the effort was made. Relationships are two-way trails — they take both sides walking toward each other.

Years later, when I returned to serve on staff, it had been about a decade since I'd first taken the course. The material was familiar, but the perspective had shifted. I wasn't just reviewing lessons; I was helping others find theirs. Watching participants struggle, grow, and discover reminded me how far I'd come — and how much I still had to learn. The network of people that Wood Badge brought into my life became one of its greatest gifts. Each course, each patrol, each story — connected into a larger fabric of leadership and service that reached far beyond any one person or patch.

There's a quiet pride in wearing those beads — not for status, but for the history and the responsibility they represent. The same feeling comes with my OA sash: gratitude for those who came before and commitment to those who will come after. They're trail markers along my Scouting journey — reminders that we're part of something enduring.

I've since watched others walk that same path. Larry, then Herb and Amanda — each with their own stories, their own lessons, their own reflections. When I stood beside them as they received their beads, I wasn't proud of them like a teacher might be, but proud for them — for what they discovered in themselves, for the chapters they added to this shared story. It's not about recognition. It's about legacy, and the greater community we build through service.

Wood Badge didn't change everything in an instant. It did so quietly, layer by layer — like water shaping stone. It gave me new tools, new friends, new understanding. It reminded me that leadership is not about being the most capable person in the room, but about seeing all the facets of the people around you and helping them shine.

In the end, it wasn't just a course. It was preparation — a stop at the camp store before the next trail segment — equipping me with perspective and purpose for the journey ahead.

And that's what made it the course that changed everything.

The Spirit of Service

When Frank Rivera approached me about the Order of the Arrow, I didn't know much about it. My troop had a couple of members at one time, but no one recent. The local chapter had been in disarray for a while — maybe that's putting it nicely. Frank, a longtime friend from the upper Keys, had served as a Cubmaster and wore his 82nd Airborne campaign hat with pride. He wanted to reestablish a foothold for the chapter in the lower Keys and thought of me to help.

He had to explain what the Order even was, and I remember listening, not fully knowing what I was getting into but feeling like I should say yes. Maybe it was his conviction, or maybe I just knew my Scouts needed something beyond the troop — another angle to see it all from. Either way, I met the camping requirement and soon found myself heading north for my Ordeal at Camp Everglades.

I'd never camped there before. The air was different, heavy with pine and stillness. The ceremony team was superb — clean movements, strong voices, regalia that carried weight and meaning. Before that, though, we were guided by our clan along a trail into the darkness. The moon was bright enough to silhouette the slash pines, and every sound felt amplified. It was cold and wet that weekend; service projects were cut short, and some Scouts had their shoes off, drying their feet in front of the kitchen oven. Others weren't prepared for the weather, so I lent out my spare clothes. By the end, when the rain pushed us under a pavilion for the closing ceremony and we wore trash bags as ponchos, it still felt powerful. The words of the ceremony lingered — layered meaning upon meaning.

Even early on, I felt like I'd already belonged there. The OA didn't change who I was; it put a name to what was already there. The call to serve, the quiet expectation to give of yourself without asking how or for what — it felt familiar, natural.

Both lodges I've been a part of have always held youth leadership in high regard. The OA's structure, with its youth-led executive committee and adult advisers who guide rather than direct, was the example I needed. It showed me that youth could carry serious responsibility when trusted to do so. Watching them plan, decide, and sometimes stumble revealed something I'd later mirror in my troop — give them space, let them try, and be there to support rather than control.

Vigil came later, and that's an honor you can't earn by checklist or tenure. You can't advocate for yourself; it simply finds you when others see your service. I remember thinking there were others more deserving, but when my name was announced that Sunday morning — sleep-deprived, thankful, and humbled — I smiled. My Vigil name, Steady Current, fit better than I could have imagined. It connects me to my sons, Ben and Matthew, through their own Vigil names — Swift Snapper and Running Deer — all creatures found near the water, each moving in its own way but carried by the same current. There's quiet humor in it too: an electronics man named for current. Clever indeed. Having Matthew as my guide that night made it even more meaningful.

Being part of the OA has always been about people — caring for them, supporting them, serving them. The cheerful part isn't about pretending everything's fine; it's about choosing joy in the act of service. That mindset shows up everywhere: in friendship, in leadership, in how we build community.

In time, my Scouts began to reflect that same spirit. The first few who were inducted were so moved by the experience that they immediately worked to help others become eligible. It became a natural cycle — youth inspiring youth, adults stepping back, and a legacy of belonging taking root. We didn't have to push it; we just supported it.

To stay a steady current is to continue, regardless of speed. It's to remain consistent and firm in purpose even when the water around you shifts. I don't think about my Vigil name often, but when I do, it's tied to the people I've walked with — friends from long ago and new Scouts just beginning their own journey. It's their energy, their excitement, that keeps me moving forward.

The OA has taught me that humility is the heart of service. Without it, we get in the way of what we really need to learn. The Spirit of Service is more than completing a project or filling a role — it's about the quiet transformation that happens when we give of ourselves for something greater.

If I had to put it into a single phrase, I'd lean on the words of Jesus: Love God. Love people. That's it. Everything else flows from there.

In the end, it was never about me. It's not even about you. It's about the collective us — the brotherhood, the shared effort, the cheerful spirit that binds us to one another in service. That's the current I hope to keep steady.

The lessons I carried from the Order of the Arrow became more than memories — they became muscle. Service, humility, and quiet consistency started to shape how I approached everything that came next. It wasn't always neat or easy. The more I tried to live out cheerful service in real life, the more I realized how messy growth can get when people, passion, and purpose collide. But even then, the current held steady, carrying me toward the next stretch of the journey — where leadership would be tested, and service would take on new meaning.

Where Growth Gets Messy

When I took over as Scoutmaster, the unit was in a season of quiet habit. Meetings ran smoothly, advancement stayed on schedule, and on the surface, things looked fine. But underneath, something didn't sit right. The Scouts weren't really leading — they were performing leadership, echoing adult instructions like lines from a script. It wasn't youth-led; it was youth-managed. I'd seen the difference. I'd experienced it through Wood Badge and the Order of the Arrow, and I knew what real ownership could look like. What we had was a façade.

As I stepped into the role, I met resistance from every angle. The adults had become comfortable with the rhythm and predictability of "how we've always done it." My effort to shift toward true youth leadership meant longer meetings, slower progress, and a lot more bumps along the way. Parents were uneasy — Scouts weren't advancing at the same pace, campouts felt less polished, and sometimes, the program looked messy. But that mess was where learning lived.

What frustrated me most wasn't the Scouts; it was the adults who couldn't see the bigger picture. They wanted to help, but in their helping, they were taking away growth. At some campouts, we had a one-to-one ratio of adults to youth. When the Scouts lagged in cleaning up, a parent would quietly step in to finish the job. It looked efficient, but it robbed the boys of the experience they needed. I knew the program's purpose wasn't comfort — it was development.

One particular weekend at Camp Sawyer stays with me. It was practically in our backyard — three miles from our meeting place — but it became one of my greatest lessons in letting go. The campsite was a disaster. Gear scattered, dishes undone, chaos everywhere.

I had a meeting on the property but managed to break away for a moment to check on the troop. Amanda met me midway and warned, "You're not going to be happy." I walked into the campsite, quiet, taking in the mess spread across camp. I sat down at the table and motioned for the boys to join me.

"This is great," I said with a grin. Their jaws dropped, confusion written all over their faces. "Your moms aren't here anymore. This is all you. I've got to get back to my meeting, but I want you to figure it out and take care of it."

Then I stood up, left them to it, and returned later to find the site spotless — proof that they could handle it when given the chance. Not because an adult stepped in, but because they were trusted to take ownership. I never had to have that conversation about campsite cleanup again.

Change rarely comes without friction. I remember walking into committee meetings with my Scoutmaster Handbook marked up with sticky notes, ready to defend every decision. The guidelines were clear — not as optional suggestions, but as the foundation of how Scouting was designed to work. Still, I was learning where firmness ends and flexibility begins — how to lead with both principle and patience. The adults were storming, but we were finding our way as a team. Slowly, we began to norm.

There were allies who began to see it. Amanda was always a steady sounding board, helping me keep the heart of it centered. And then there was Alex — a Scout who transferred in that fall and was elected SPL by December. At his first Court of Honor, he stood before the troop and said, "Tell your parents to step out of the kitchen. You're cleaning up." That one moment said everything. The spark had caught. The youth were beginning to lead, and some adults were finally starting to follow.

Over time, I learned that trust is a process — one that requires more patience than control. I stopped chasing perfection and started watching for progress. There were many times I had to step back and remind myself: you don't have to fix this right now. Growth doesn't happen on command. It happens in time, through effort, and often through failure.

Looking back, I realize how much faith was woven through those moments — not just spiritual faith, but faith in the program, in the process, and in the people. I had to believe that the methods laid out in those handbooks weren't just theoretical ideals, but lived truths written by those who had seen it work. I had to believe that if I held to the vision and stayed the course, the growth would come.

Humility wasn't always my strong suit then. I saw my role as the keeper of the program, the one responsible for ensuring it was delivered as it was meant to be. There were times I even offered my seat to those who disagreed, ready to let them take on the responsibility if they thought they could do better. But in hindsight, even that stubbornness was part of my own growing process — obedience without full understanding. I was living the Scout Oath and Law, not perfectly, but with sincerity.

Now, with distance, I can see how right the timing was. I had said yes, been trained, and witnessed youth-led Scouting in its pure form. When the unit needed change, I was equipped — even if I didn't yet realize it. The struggle taught me patience, trust, and the quiet confidence that transformation takes time. It's not about forcing results but creating the environment where growth can happen — where both Scouts and leaders can discover what they're truly capable of.

"Where Growth Gets Messy" wasn't just about a troop learning to lead; it was about me learning to let go of certainty and lead through faith. It was about trusting the process, believing in the unseen potential of others, and finding that, often, God's work looks a lot like a messy campsite before it becomes a story worth telling.

42

The Lesson of Letting Go

It's funny, the things we think matter most when we start leading. For me, it began with something as small as a T-shirt. I wanted every Scout to keep it tucked in when wearing the Class B uniform. It was about pride and discipline — lessons I'd carried from military life. But the more I pushed it, the more resistance I met. Some complied, most didn't. What I thought was a standard became a stumbling block. It caused friction where there didn't need to be any. I was learning the hard way that control isn't the same as leadership.

I had zoomed too far into the weeds. Somewhere along the way, I lost sight of the why. It wasn't about tucked shirts — it was about pride, ownership, respect — and I hadn't taken the time to connect those dots for the Scouts. I realized I had to be more selective in where I invested my energy. The lesson wasn't just in letting go of control; it was learning how to see what really mattered.

At summer camp one year, that truth hit harder than I expected. A well-meaning parent kept reminding the Scouts to grab their water bottles, over and over. Finally, midweek, I called her out — gently but publicly. "You need to let the SPL do his job," I said. She bristled, saying she was just trying to keep them safe. I replied, "Then wait until they start walking off before you step in. Give him a chance to prepare his troop for the day." She walked away upset, and I got the silent treatment most of the day. I don't usually condone calling someone out in front of others, but in that moment, it was necessary. The SPL needed to see that I trusted him and expected others to do the same. And he rose to it.

Sometimes letting go meant literally sitting on my hands — forcing myself to watch instead of jump in. I had to let them try, even if it took longer or looked sloppy. I could encourage from the sidelines, remind them they knew how, ask one Scout to teach another — but I had to resist the urge to "fix" everything. Perfection had been my measure; growth became my new goal.

One campout at Sawyer stands out. Ben was Quartermaster, and he and the SPL weren't seeing eye to eye during pack-up. Things were getting loud. Ben was pulling gear out of the trailer that had just been loaded, claiming it wasn't in the right place. The SPL was frustrated — ready to just make it fit and go home. I pulled him aside. "Did he say why he's doing it?" I asked. "Yeah," he said, "but I just want to get done." I looked at him and asked, "What's the job of the Quartermaster?" He answered, and I nodded. "Then he's doing his job. Maybe we support him this time, and figure out later how not to go through this again." The SPL thought for a second, nodded back, and went to help. It wasn't perfect, but it was progress — and that mattered more.

Patience was tested often. I could have stepped in, but if I did it once, I'd have to do it every time. Learning restraint meant trusting them to figure it out — to learn by doing, not by watching me do it for them. And when they succeeded, the joy was different. When you rule, it's for you. When you enable, it's for them. Their success became my pride. Their failures became my responsibility — a call to find better ways to support and empower them.

Faith crept into that space quietly, even when I didn't recognize it at the time. Learning to let go in Scouting mirrored learning to let go in life — to trust that God was leading, even when I didn't see the full picture. It's not a one-time lesson; it's one I still wrestle with. But that's the point, isn't it? Growth doesn't happen in the moments we control. It happens in the ones we release.

Looking back, I wouldn't have wanted it to be easier. The struggle made the lesson stick. Just as the Scouts learn by trial and error, so do we as adults. We learn to admit we don't have all the answers and to model the process of figuring it out. That's what leadership really is — not knowing everything, but trusting enough to let others discover it for themselves.

Because in the end, letting go isn't about walking away. It's about making space — for others to rise, for God to move, and for growth to take root in places our control could never reach.

Passing the Torch

I once heard that good leaders work to put themselves out of a job. I didn't live with a succession chart taped to the wall, but I did feel the pull toward relief: fewer hats in the unit, clearer roles in the district, less of the "do it anyway" because a committee couldn't see the vision yet. In a small, often-overlooked district, it felt normal to carry extra weight. Still, without saying it out loud, I was preparing others. Kevin Creighton took IOLS and Scoutmaster-specific. He wasn't eager for a title, but he was steady, thoughtful, present.

My first big hand off didn't go as planned. I stepped down as district camping chair after we'd launched a youth-chief program — built to give young leaders a district-level proving ground and to model youth-led for every troop. My replacement scrapped it almost immediately. It wasn't perfect; it was, however, alive. I was angry. Then he relocated, and the job boomeranged back to me. The trust, though — that fragile bridge we'd built with the youth — had been kicked out from under them. In quiet resolve, our PLC decided we wouldn't support district events without youth representation. No grandstanding — just a line drawn for principle's sake. The program had borrowed from the Scoutmaster Camporee Chief progression; losing it left a mark.

Keys Scouting has its own geography and gravity. Wood Badge-trained adults were scarce; NYLT graduates, rarer still. Getting youth engaged at the lodge level was a four-hour round trip — hard to sustain. We tried to build analogs locally. Some took. Some didn't. People embrace what they understand; sometimes they prefer what they know over what they're willing to learn. I learned to meet folks where they were and keep serving.

When it came time to leave the Keys, it happened fast — faster than my ideal of a carefully staged hand off. Months earlier, a whisper: Time for change. I thought it meant a radical shift — electronics and radar traded for youth pastoring. I was willing to move entirely. Doors didn't open that way, but they opened all the same: job offer, house closed on December 23, new house closed on December 28. That wasn't coincidence; it was orchestration.

Kevin, with his "Brady Bunch" family — three sons, three daughters — had always weighed Scouting against home wisely. Then he stood up. No fanfare, just presence. The troop kept moving forward: boys leading, adults supporting, a sense of family intact. Years later, on a business trip, I "happened" to be in the Keys the week of a Court of Honor. I sat in the back and watched. It was stronger than when I left — more Scouts, more adults than I remembered. Kevin said what needed saying and let the youth own the rest. Pride, gratitude, and confirmation washed over me. Legacy wasn't about my fingerprints staying visible; it was about the shape holding when my hands were gone.

Wood Badge had taught me the rhythm of progression — participant to Troop Guide to roles that refine both skill and humility. Jamboree taught something different — selection, trust, and rising to meet a need. Between the two, I came to see that leadership is temporary; stewardship is the constant. You carry the weight until another shoulder arrives — willing, not necessarily ready. I think of the OA ceremonies: you endure what is yours to bear until someone steps forward and takes the burden. The moment is simple, almost quiet, but holy all the same.

Not everything I built survived. Not everything should. What endured were convictions: youth at the forefront, adults as scaffolding, and a troop culture sturdy enough to outlast personalities. Now and then a note reaches me — "Thank you for holding firm on boy-led. We see the difference." I smile, not because it proves me right, but because it means the boys learned to lead where it counts.

Micah 6:8 hums under all of it — do justice, love mercy, walk humbly. And the Lord's own words about coming to serve, not to be served, anchor the rest (Mark 10:45). Obedience sometimes looks like stepping up; sometimes it looks like stepping aside. In both, the work is God's.

My Vigil name — Steady Current — reminds me that movement isn't always dramatic. It's faithful, patient, persistent — carrying others at the pace they can manage, toward the place they're meant to arrive.

I won't tell the next chapter here. It's enough to say that sitting at that Court of Honor, I felt a quiet release and a gentle readiness. The torch hadn't gone out. It simply changed hands, and the light reached further than before.

 Trail Marker II -
Stepping Forward in Scouting

Service often begins with a simple yes — a willingness to show up and fill a need. Over time, that yes becomes something deeper. What starts as helping becomes leading, and what begins as duty becomes calling. In Scouting, that shift happens quietly through campfires, meetings, and the moments that stretch patience and purpose. Leadership proves less about control and more about trust — learning to listen, to guide lightly, and to let others find their own footing.

As this chapter of service closes, the trail bends toward something new. The call to serve doesn't end; it changes direction. What was once outward leadership turns inward — toward discernment, quiet listening, and faith in what comes next. The same God who urged you forward now invites you to pause, breathe, and prepare for the next climb.

> *"For even the Son of Man did not come to be served, but to serve, and to give His life as a ransom for many." — Mark 10:45*

Reflective Questions

1. When have your own small yeses grown into something far beyond what you expected?
2. What has leading others taught you about humility and patience?
3. How can you create space for others to grow — even when it means stepping back?
4. Where might God be inviting you to shift from leading to listening?

Closing Prayer

Lord my God, thank You for the seasons that have stretched and shaped me.
Help me to serve with grace, to release what I cannot hold, and to trust that You are guiding the steps I do not yet see.
As I move from leading to listening, let my heart stay open to Your will and steady in Your peace.
Amen.

Listening to Leave

There are times when obedience asks for pause instead of progress. This part walks through the tension of release — the quiet grace of stepping away when everything familiar calls you to remain. In that stillness, God's voice becomes clearer, reminding us that leaving can also be an act of faith.

Chapters within this segment:

The Restless Season

The weeks after leaving the Keys were a blur. I'd been making weekend trips north with a U-Haul trailer, filling a storage unit one load at a time, never quite sure where anything belonged yet. Seventeen years in one place — the same drive, the same radar site, the same community I'd poured myself into — had left me tired and ready for change. Still, to leave the family I helped create was bittersweet.

We stayed with my mother-in-law while everything fell into place. She insisted we take her room. Amanda would rise early so I could have a hot breakfast — eggs and spinach before my Peloton ride — then I'd head out for the long drive to work. It was near Christmas, and though we were grateful, It felt like a pause between what was and what would be. We weren't settled; we were simply waiting for the next sentence to start.

When we finally closed on the house and started to unpack, I felt that familiar itch. For almost two decades in the Keys, service had been part of my life — Scouting, church, community. Now that the boxes had found homes, I needed to as well. I began looking for a troop, and for a church with a youth group. I figured my experience still had purpose; maybe I could help another unit grow the way ours once had.

Pulling into the unfamiliar church parking lot, I wasn't sure what I'd find. I knew the uniform would speak before I did, so I made sure my knots and Wood Badge beads were there — a visible sign of commitment — of time already served and a heart still willing to invest. Walking through those doors as the "old guy without a kid in the program" was awkward, but familiar. When the Scoutmaster asked what I wanted to do, I didn't have a plan. I just asked, "What do you need?"

The next morning, I sent an email:

"I had the pleasure of attending the troop meeting last night and I feel like there is a fit for me somewhere in the unit... I feel my calling is to serve — specifically the youth of my community. Now that we have moved into Melbourne, this is now my community."

At the time, it felt simple — an introduction, a next step. Looking back, it carried more than that. It was my first written act of belonging in a new place, a bridge between what had been and what would come next.

That Sunday, we walked into Wesley. We'd already decided to visit before I ever learned, at the troop meeting earlier that week, that it would be Scout Sunday. The service itself wasn't about Scouting — just a brief acknowledgment of the Scouts who were there. Still, the timing felt like one of those quiet nods from God. He'd used Scout Sunday once before to bring me back to church, and this time it felt like a reminder: "I'm still here."

Through it all, my prayer life stayed conversational. I talked with God throughout the day — small thoughts, quick thanks, quiet questions. I didn't need formal words; I just needed connection. Amanda's steadiness kept me grounded. She was dealing with her own stresses, yet somehow remained the rock I leaned on. I try to return that strength, but I still feel I fall short in comparison.

Looking back, I realize that restlessness wasn't impatience — it was transition. Months earlier I'd heard that whisper, time to change, and I'd taken it to mean career. Maybe it was bigger than that. Maybe it was God preparing me for this very season — one that would ask for trust more than direction.

I couldn't have named it then, but that's what this chapter of life became: uncharted territory. A stretch between leaving and arriving. A space where serving wasn't about position or program but about being willing, once again, to listen for what came next.

Out of Step

I said yes because that's what I do. When another Scouter reached out asking me to serve as District Camping Chair, it felt like an easy way to contribute — ideas, experience, and willingness to help. But within weeks, the weight of that yes began to feel misplaced. My phone buzzed at summer camp with an email telling me that I was now the point of contact for the Cub Family Campout (CFCO). No conversation, no check-in — just a declaration. I was standing in the Florida heat at Camp La-No-Che, half amused and half offended, reading it twice to be sure.

I drafted several replies, each one a little sharper than the last, before sending something that balanced truth with restraint. I wasn't available that weekend. I didn't have the local network. I didn't even know most of the pack leaders yet. Still, I tried to start a plan — proposing themes, schedules, and the kind of structure that had made our old district events successful. The silence on the other end said plenty. When I followed up, the response I got back wasn't collaboration; it was confirmation that they'd already moved ahead without me. They wanted something easy, something recycled. "We'll just use what worked a few years ago." That was the moment I knew I was out of step with where the district was — and maybe with what God was asking of me.

The cliques were real. Roundtable felt like walking into someone else's living room mid-conversation. Names, inside jokes, sideways looks. I tried, but I couldn't shake the sense that I didn't belong. Within a month of that CFCO exchange, I resigned. Not in anger — just clarity. I wasn't the right person for that moment. Maybe the district wasn't ready for the kind of energy I wanted to bring. Or maybe I wasn't ready to slow down and listen first.

But old habits die hard. I kept looking for places to serve. I offered to help with a Scouts BSA Camporee, thinking it might be a fresh start. My hope was to build an event led by Scouts themselves — youth planning, youth running, adults quietly supporting. At least one Scoutmaster didn't agree. "My Scouts aren't ready for that," he told me. I knew what he meant, but what I heard was, They'll never be ready if we don't let them try. Once again, I found myself seeing a program that wasn't there yet. I could picture what it might become, but not everyone wanted to look that far ahead.

The same pattern played out at church. I'd offered to help with the youth group, only to be told there were enough volunteers already. "But maybe," they said, "you could start something for the young adults?" So I tried. Most weeks it was just Tommy and me in the cavernous fellowship hall, two or three people at best, all sitting around tables meant for dozens. They wanted a class, something to attend — not something they had to own. I remembered what my own youth group had been — alive, driven, ours. This wasn't that. I kept showing up, hoping momentum would come, but it never did. Eventually, it became clear I was trying to spark something God hadn't asked me to ignite.

All of it — the district work, the camporee, the church nights — started to blend into one lesson. I was learning that eagerness and timing don't always walk together. Sometimes you can be right in what you see and still wrong in when you step. Those months humbled me. They made me slow down, listen longer, and recognize that leadership isn't just about motion — it's about discernment.

It took time, but the frustration softened into peace. I began to see this season not as wasted effort, but as wilderness — a quiet stretch meant to strip away my need to fix, lead, or prove. God wasn't punishing my enthusiasm; He was shaping my patience. Through those small defeats, I learned that being out of step didn't mean being off the path. It just meant I was being prepared for what was still to come.

TRAIL MARKER III -
Anchored in Surrender

There comes a point in every journey when forward motion slows — not because the path has ended, but because the next turn requires listening more than leading. This season of surrender isn't about giving up; it's about giving over. When the familiar patterns fade and your hands feel empty, that's often where God begins to steady the heart for what's next.

In these in-between places, restlessness meets grace. The desire to keep doing softens into the discipline of being. When life feels out of step, the Spirit whispers a quieter way — one that trades urgency for trust. It's here, in the stillness, that faith is refined and identity is reanchored.

Surrender doesn't erase calling; it restores it. Anchoring in God's presence renews clarity for the path ahead, reminding us that strength isn't found in striving, but in reliance. The same God who once called you into motion now calls you to rest — not to stop, but to stand firm in His peace.

"Since we live by the Spirit, let us keep in step with the Spirit." — *Galatians 5:25*

Reflective Questions

1. Where in your life are you being invited to release control and simply trust God's timing?
2. How have restlessness and waiting shaped your understanding of faith?
3. What does "being in step with the Spirit" look like in this season of your journey?
4. How can stillness become a place of renewal rather than resistance?

Closing Prayer

Lord, teach me the strength found in surrender.
When my plans falter and the path feels uncertain, anchor me in Your presence.
Help me trust the pace You set — to rest, to listen, and to follow when You say go.
May stillness draw me closer to Your will and renew my spirit for the journey ahead.
Amen.

Segment IV -

Rooted Again

After the silence comes renewal. What once felt like loss becomes fertile soil for rediscovery — of joy, calling, and presence. This part finds peace in slower days and purpose in steady trust. To be rooted again is to see how God restores not what was, but what can now grow deeper.

Chapters within this segment:

Steady in the Stillness

It didn't come all at once.

There wasn't a single sunrise or conversation that defined the moment. It was more like the tide — a steady, patient pull that reshaped the shoreline of my heart.

I had learned that sometimes God doesn't shout or shake; He stills. The restlessness that once drove me to fix, to do, to fill every need began to quiet. I still showed up at meetings, still stood ready when a weekend needed one more leader — but I no longer felt the pull to take on what wasn't mine. What I did take on, I did with purpose. My journal pages began to reflect that shift — less about what needed to change and more about what was being refined.

At first, I thought I was simply pruning — saying no to things that didn't fit anymore. But it turned out to be something deeper. It was seeding. The things I said no to created room for what mattered most: youth-led growth, space for others to serve, time to listen.

There were quiet confirmations — verses that met me twice in the same week, a sermon that echoed a prayer I'd written days earlier. "There are no coincidences," Gibbs would say, and I smiled at how right he was.

In stepping back, I found more than rest; I found alignment. My identity wasn't tied to the titles or tasks, but to the why — I love God, I love people, and I act on it the best way I know how. That's what was being restored.

This was obedience not in motion, but in stillness.

Faithfulness without fanfare.
A calm resolve that what was next would unfold in His time, not mine.

If I could put that season into a single sentence, it would read:
"I stopped chasing what was and started preparing for what could be."

The storm had passed, but the anchor held. The water was still, the current steady.
And in that stillness, I could finally hear again.

As the dawn stretched across a field of dew-drenched tents, I stood quietly — not
as the leader this time, but simply as a man grateful to still be called to serve. The
sun rose, slow and sure, lighting a new day — one that would soon take root.

> *"Trust in the Lord with all your heart and lean not on your own understanding."*
> *— Proverbs 3:5*

Closing Prayer – Steady in the Stillness

Lord,
thank You for teaching me that stillness is not weakness,
> *but trust.*
For every season You have allowed to slow my pace,
> *for every burden You've asked me to set down,*
> *thank You for the space to listen again.*
Help me remember that obedience is not always in the doing,
> *sometimes it is simply in the being —*
> *being faithful, being present, being Yours.*
Anchor my heart in Your timing,
> *steady my spirit when I reach to control what only You can guide.*
May the quiet I've found here grow into readiness
> *for whatever You choose to plant next.*
In the calm of this morning,
> *with the dew still fresh on the tents and the light breaking through,*
> *I choose to trust that what You begin in stillness*
> *You will bring to life in Your perfect time.*
Amen.

Rediscovery

After the stillness that followed letting go, I started to find steadiness again. It began simply — going to church, helping with the troop. Nothing new or dramatic, just returning to places that had always mattered. Showing up gave me space to breathe. It reminded me that faith doesn't always begin with a calling; sometimes it begins by being present.

For a long time I had stepped forward because no one else would. This time I learned to stand only where I was meant to, where my heart and gifts fit the need. I didn't need to lead from the front or carry every task. I could follow, support, and encourage. The leadership lessons I had taught for years about growing from self-awareness to shared responsibility started to make more sense when I stopped trying to hold everything together myself.

I thought often about the parable of the sower. In earlier years I had scattered effort everywhere, believing every opportunity deserved attention. Now I paid attention to where things actually grew. When something showed life, I stayed with it. When it struggled or closed off, I let it be. That wasn't giving up — it was trust. Not every field was mine to tend, and learning that brought peace that striving never could.

Faith began to grow again through ordinary moments. Reading a few verses before bed. Writing when I needed to make sense of something. Seeing familiar faces at church start to greet us by name. Watching young Scouts find the courage to ask for help. Each was a quiet reminder that belief and service belong together.

If I were to picture that time, I'd see a small seedling breaking through dark soil beside a trickle of water. The seedling is me, still growing, learning where to put down roots. The water is God, constant and moving, shaping the ground even when I don't see it. I didn't realize then how much was happening beneath the surface. Looking back now, I know — there's never nothing going on. God is always at work, even when we can't see it.

64

The Return

There's a feeling that comes when you catch sight of a campfire in the distance. You don't need to run toward it or call out — you simply know it's there, steady and sure, waiting to welcome you back into its warmth. That's how I feel now, looking back at the words I wrote years ago in a season when I thought I was finding my way home to God.

At the time, I was watching Confessions of a Prodigal Son. In the film, a student is assigned to write an essay reflecting on the story, and I decided to take on the same assignment myself. What I didn't realize was that it would become one of the most honest pieces I had ever written — a reflection of where I was and where I hoped to be.

Prodigal Son?

Thinking about the story of the prodigal son and how it could be related to my life. There was a time in my life when I was highly active in the church. My grandparents would pick me up at home and take me to church on Sundays. As I got older, I was able to join the church youth group and go through confirmation class. I would stop in after school on Wednesdays and help set up for the weekly dinner and Bible study. I was active with the church's missions committee. Then came graduation and my departure to the military.

In basic training, going to church on Sundays was a retreat from the drills, the ironing of clothes into six-inch squares, the cleaning, and the Texas heat. At tech school, the importance of church went dormant. Besides getting married back home in the church I grew up in, the only other times I remember attending church was when I was deployed to Bosnia until we left the military and moved to the Keys. Even when I visited home and intended on stopping in on a Sunday morning or Christmas Eve service, I somehow managed to have an excuse.

I really do not know why. It was not because I stopped believing in God. I had faith. Most people do not know that Amanda and I only knew each other two months before we were married. I still remember telling my dad that there was something different about her; that was a feeling I had I could not explain but trusted instead. William was born and becoming a father gave a new perspective and understanding of my dad and, in a way, God. Then came Ben and Matthew — seven weeks premature. I think then was when I began being mindful to have faith that things would work out — trust in God.

I think God has been speaking to me. Not the burning-bush voice from the heavens, but in a way I cannot quite describe. The first was the strong belief I needed to join the Air Force. Had I not, I would not have met Amanda. I already told a little bit of our story — I feel as if I was meant to meet her. Twice in the Air Force I can remember being somewhere and thinking, I will live here someday. Both came to fruition. We were stationed in California, but first we had visited there on vacation. The other is where we are now in the Keys, and the feeling came when I was here evaluating the radar site I currently work at.

I have had a couple other stronger occurrences of God speaking to me. The first was leaving the military. I managed to find myself on the "fat-boy" program for busting weight. I also managed to injure my knee in a freak accident during an intramural soccer game. I was in a place I could not work out effectively and needed to reduce my weight. No matter what I did I just could not get off the program. Then came the day I was placed on the list to be discharged as part of a downsizing in manning. I panicked. I went to the base chaplain for comfort. I had a wife and three boys, and I was worried about what to do. On my walk back, a calmness came over me and, in my head, I heard myself say, "I am an electronic technician, and I can find a job." In three days, I had a job offer here in the Keys.

So, what brought me back to church? Scout Sunday. Yes, Scouting was another gut feeling. I can recall weeks thinking about volunteering as a leader before bed and discussing it with Amanda. February came and it was Scout Sunday. Church that morning was reminiscent of being back in my youth and while this church is much smaller than the church I grew up in, it somehow had the same feel. We started attending regularly and became members; the boys were baptized. We tried having a youth group and youth Bible study — it worked for a while.

I sold the idea to myself that it was because of my work schedule, Scouts, and family time as to why we slowed our attendance at church. But on reflection, there is one thing that sticks out that upset me and caused me to distance from the church. The youth group wanted to have a lock-in in the Fellowship Hall over Thanksgiving break, and the pastor at the time had feelings that the boys did not show enough respect and told me they could not do it. Most of the youth group were also Scouts, so instead of fighting the decision I decided I would just work with the youth I had in the troop and allow the youth group to deteriorate. I was stretching myself trying to work with both groups, and it allowed me to give better focus. Part of me still regrets it. The church has not had another youth group and since has even lost younger families and is slowly dying.

About five weeks ago God spoke to me again. For the second time I felt the severe calmness and words in my head, "Time to change." I was on my way to the blimp site and was running early, so I pulled over on the side of the road to watch the birds. When I told Amanda, I used the phrase "different line of work" when I thought all I meant was not working at the blimp site. Of course, she called me on it and asked what type of work I wanted to do. Not knowing exactly but knowing the passion I have working with the Scouts, I said something working with mentoring youth. Conversation went on and the idea of going back to school came up. "Weird thought, but maybe not so — what about a youth pastor?" I said to Amanda.

Since then, I have been working this Kairos journal daily as best as I can and trying to be in the Word — focusing more on gratitude, praying, learning scripture, and trying to listen more for God in the daily ongoings. I have not been perfect, and that is okay. I have been feeling better at work and at home. There has been a different focus in my mind. When I have talked to others about what is going on with me, I can feel the smile on my face it is so big. I am getting goosebumps typing this now. I cannot say for sure I will end up being a youth pastor, and I am fine with that too. I am excited for the possible change and the continued servitude I can provide this world — knowing now I am, and have been, doing it in the name of God — in Jesus.

Am I a prodigal son? In some ways, I believe so. In others, I never stopped believing, so no. These last few weeks though, with how things have been, I almost feel as if God is celebrating my returned focus to Him and the church. There are other parts of me that, looking back, feel as if all that I have been through was intended to place me here now with the right experiences and skills needed and God just said, "It is time." I am still a work in progress — and it is good.

When I read those words now, I can still feel the wonder that stirred in me then — but I also see how little I understood what that "change" would truly mean. I thought it was about a title, maybe a calling to serve youth in a new way. Instead, it was about becoming someone through whom God could reach them.

At that time, I believed I was walking back toward Him. Now I know I was simply walking with Him all along — through the quiet, the confusion, the miles between duty stations, and every Scout meeting that rekindled faith in small, steady ways.

Grace, I've come to realize, isn't about being welcomed home. It's about discovering that you were never sent away. Like a Scout learning by experience instead of instruction, I needed to live the distance to understand belonging.

I am still imperfect. I still wrestle with direction and timing. Yet every time I've trusted the nudge — "Time to change," "Do this," "Go there" — I've found myself standing exactly where I was meant to be. None of it was coincidence; all of it was guidance.

The younger me wrote, "I am still a work in progress — and it is good." I hold to that still. Maybe the progress isn't about perfecting faith but about letting it steady me — like the constant light of that campfire in the distance. It doesn't demand I hurry; it only reminds me that I'm already home.

 TRAIL MARKER IV -
Rooted Again

After the storm and the stillness comes something quieter but stronger — growth taking hold beneath the surface. Renewal rarely arrives with drama; it begins in small moments of rediscovery, when you realize your calling wasn't lost, only your footing. God was preparing the soil in the waiting, readying you for what comes next.

Rooting again means trusting the ground under your feet — seeing where faith has carried you and where it still calls you to stand. Renewal isn't about returning to who you were, but becoming who you were meant to be. What was surrendered now bears fruit, what was broken begins to mend, and the same God who carried you through stillness now calls you to stand firm, grounded and ready for what's ahead.

> *"So then, just as you received Christ Jesus as Lord, continue to live your lives in Him, rooted and built up in Him, strengthened in the faith as you were taught, and overflowing with thankfulness." — Colossians 2:6–7*

Reflective Questions

1. What signs of renewal have you noticed in seasons that once felt like endings?
2. How has rediscovering God's presence changed the way you see your purpose?
3. What does it mean for you to be "rooted" in faith rather than restless in pursuit?
4. Where is God calling you to stand firm right now, even before the next step is clear?

Closing Prayer

Lord, thank You for the gift of renewal after surrender.
Help me recognize how Your quiet work has strengthened my roots and deepened my faith.
Let peace and gratitude guide my steps as I walk in awareness of Your presence.
May I remain grounded in Your truth and ready for whatever You are preparing next.
Amen.

The Path Ahead

The journey doesn't end — it unfolds. This final part looks toward what's next with open hands and steady faith. It is about passing wisdom forward, serving with gratitude, and walking into the unknown with confidence in the One who guides every step.

The path ahead isn't about arrival, but about walking faithfully — one step at a time, guided by the One who leads on.

Chapters within this segment:

A Living Legacy

"And the things you have heard me say in the presence of many witnesses entrust to reliable people who will also be qualified to teach others." — 2 Timothy 2:2

There's a story told in Scouting circles about a boy in the London fog. He stopped to help a stranger find his way, asked nothing in return, and walked away having no idea that his small act would ripple across the world. That moment helped inspire the founding of the Boy Scouts, but the boy's name was never recorded. His service spoke for itself. That's the kind of legacy I hope to live — unseen, uncredited, but enduring.

My life has been shaped by those who quietly invested in me: my parents and grandparents, Francie, and so many others whose faithfulness left a mark far deeper than words. I am, in many ways, their living echo. And now, as I look back over the path I've walked, I see how those echoes multiply — not because I planned it, but because grace and service have a way of continuing on their own.

When I returned to visit my old troop, I tried to sneak in quietly, hoping to blend into the back of the room. It didn't work. The Scouts found me immediately, and what I saw filled me with a pride I can't quite put into words. The troop was alive and thriving — full of laughter, warmth, and family. Watching them, I realized that legacy isn't a monument. It's a movement that continues in the small ways people love and lead each other.

Over the years, I've learned that mentoring isn't a title or a program — it's a posture. It's treating others as people who matter, listening to that quiet tug to act when someone needs to be seen, and trusting that God will place you where you're needed. Influence happens when you guide instead of control, suggest instead of demand, love instead of lead from ego. Control tries to preserve what we built; influence trusts others to carry it forward.

I never set out to leave a legacy. He > Me has always been my compass. Legacy became something that happened in the background of obedience — an echo of God's work, not my own. My hope is that those who've crossed my path felt seen, safe, and encouraged to do the same for someone else.

It was never about the legacy, the awards, or the trinkets. At some point, there was a shift — from accomplishment to alignment, from recognition to relationship, from striving to serving. What remains is the peace of knowing that I've planted seeds for a forest I may never see, and that's enough.

The Path Ahead

"I press on toward the goal for the prize of the upward call of God in Christ Jesus."
— Philippians 3:14

It wasn't planned, at least not by me. One moment I was in casual conversation about Josh stepping down, and the next, I heard my own voice offering to take on Scoutmaster again. I hadn't mapped it out or weighed it in prayer for weeks. It just came out — that same familiar pattern of following a nudge before I felt ready. And here I am again, stepping into a role that feels both familiar and new, trusting that my gut — or maybe the quiet whisper of the Spirit — knew what it was doing all along.

This time, though, it feels different. The first time, I fought for the position. This time, I offered — and it was accepted. There's humility in that shift. Faith and service have always been woven together in my life, but now the thread feels stronger, more deliberate. I've learned that pressing on doesn't mean striving harder; it means moving faithfully. Sometimes that means speaking up, sometimes stepping back, and sometimes simply showing up and being present.

I'm careful not to criticize what came before. I know how that can feel. But what I see now in Scouts and parents alike is a focus on outcomes — badges, ranks, Eagle. I want to return to what brought me here in the first place: the adventure, the journey, the growth that happens along the way. I want these boys to stay because they want to, because they see purpose in the journey — and in each other. That's the path I'm chasing: one where faith, fun, and formation walk hand in hand.

When I look out over what's ahead, it feels like standing on a ridge after a long climb — seeing the trail stretch far beyond where sight can reach. I can't walk it alone. I may never see its end. And yet, I press on. My mission isn't the distant horizon; it's in the now. The conversations, the laughter, the hard days, the moments of grace — this is the work. Eternity will take care of itself.

I've learned that my gut and heart are usually aligned long before my head catches up. There are still fears — of being misunderstood, of progress not coming fast enough, of not relating to this new generation. But when those doubts creep in, I remember the simple truth: He's got it, and He's already given me what I need to do it. My gifts, my heart, my people — all in place for this moment. What has been seen cannot be unseen. And once you've seen God move through your life, you can't help but move forward differently.

If The First Yes was about courage and calling, The Path Ahead is about trust and purpose. The faces around me have changed, but the reason I serve hasn't. My compass is steadied by quiet reflection, by Amanda's grounding presence, by Scripture, by early morning runs where I breathe and listen. I don't know how far this path goes or what the next rise will reveal. But I do know this: the call is still the same — to walk faithfully, to lead humbly, and to keep pressing toward the upward call.

And if someone were to walk beside me and ask how they'll know they're on the right path, I'd tell them what I keep telling myself: trust your gut — it got you where you were meant to be.

Send Me

Readiness doesn't always come with a road map. Sometimes it's simply a quiet trust — a willingness to step forward without knowing where the path will lead. "Here am I, send me." Those words have echoed in my heart for years, yet only now do I fully understand what they mean. It isn't about confidence or clarity; it's about faith that the next step will appear when it's time. Ready, willing, trusting — open-ended, without destination defined.

Looking back, I can see a lifetime of stacked "send me" moments — the decisions that shaped the path I didn't expect. Military service. Marriage. Leaving the Keys. Taking on new roles and responsibilities. Each time, there was no guarantee of success, only a quiet assurance that I wasn't walking alone. Marriage, especially, was the leap that continues to teach me what it means to be sent — a daily act of faith, commitment, and shared purpose.

Being sent doesn't always mean going somewhere new. More often, it means living out love where you already are. There is a daily mission to live like Christ — to love God and love people — and that's a call that never expires. Most missions happen in our own communities, in our homes, in the small, consistent ways we show up for others.

Amanda and I have walked this out together since 1996. We've stepped in faith, sometimes stumbling, sometimes soaring, always learning. She was the first Scout volunteer in our family, and she's still the one who tells me, "Go," when she sees that spark in me. I support her in the same way, because we've learned that being sent isn't a solo mission — it's a shared one.

Over time, I've come to see that humility and obedience are woven into this calling. Being sent may mean heading toward a place not yet revealed on the map. It's about letting go and trusting that God's plan may not always match your own, yet it will always be good. And when I hesitate, history reminds me — He's never failed me yet.

Service that endures is never about recognition. It's about giving for the benefit of others, the kind of giving that continues long after you've stepped away. Like the candles of a Christmas Eve service — one light igniting another, spreading warmth and glow beyond what one could do alone.

I've seen that spirit in others too. Pastor Ryan — unashamed, genuine, and passionate — living proof that being sent means bringing your whole self to the work. I've seen it in countless Scouts who took on roles they weren't sure they were ready for, who learned that doing their best was enough. One in particular comes to mind — smaller than his peers, unsure if he belonged as Senior Patrol Leader. He gave everything he had, 100 percent. And that's all anyone should ever be asked to give.

If I could tell the next generation one thing, it would be this: Don't wait to feel ready. If something stirs in your heart, lean into it. Step forward. Be willing to be sent — and when you do, know that you're not alone.

This story isn't finished. It never will be. It's an invitation to keep walking — to keep saying yes when the call comes, even if it looks nothing like what you imagined.

The call isn't just mine. It's yours too.

Wherever you stand, there is someone who needs your light, your steadiness, your willingness to serve. You don't have to know where the path leads — only that you're willing to walk it. So listen for the quiet whisper. When it comes — and it will — may you have the courage to answer, "Here am I. Send me."

Trail Marker V -
The Path Ahead

The journey of faith doesn't end when the path grows familiar — it deepens. Every experience, every season of surrender and renewal, prepares you for what comes next. The call to serve continues, shaped now by wisdom, humility, and gratitude. It's not about starting over, but walking forward with clearer purpose and steadier faith.

This final stretch of the trail reminds us that legacy isn't measured in recognition, but in the lives we've touched, the lessons we've shared, and the light we've carried. Each act of service, no matter how small, becomes part of something larger — a living reflection of God's work in and through us.

The path ahead isn't about knowing every turn. It's about trusting that the same God who guided every step before will keep leading on. So walk forward — not with fear, but with faith; not for your own glory, but to honor the One who called you. The journey continues, and so does His purpose in you.

> *"I press on toward the goal for the prize of the upward call of God in Christ Jesus."*
> *— Philippians 3:14*

Reflective Questions

1. How has your understanding of service evolved as you've walked this path?
2. What legacy of faith and leadership do you hope to leave those who follow?
3. Where might God be inviting you to press on — not out of striving, but out of trust?
4. How can you remain open and ready to say "Send me" when the next call comes?

Closing Prayer

Lord, thank You for every step, every lesson, and every life touched along this journey.
Help me walk forward with courage and humility, pressing on toward Your purpose.
May my life reflect Your light and inspire others to serve with faith and love.
Amen.

Bridge

The fire had cooled, yet its glow remained — steady, patient, and alive.

From the ashes of one season rose a quiet light: the light of brotherhood.

In the Order of the Arrow we call it cheerful service — that bond formed when hearts align in purpose and hands find work worth doing together.

That same spirit carried me from rebuilding in Melbourne to reflection — back through every lesson the trail had offered and every person who shaped it. The glow of that fellowship still warms the path behind me and points toward what endures beyond any single role or season.

Before stepping forward again came a pause — gratitude for every mile, every friend, every spark still burning.

And with that light still guiding the way, the trail turned toward its next question: Why do we keep walking?

Encampment –
Why We Scout

"For even the Son of Man did not come to be served, but to serve." — Mark 10:45

People sometimes ask why I'm still here.

My sons have aged out, my uniform's faded, and I've worn about every hat Scouting offers. I could have stepped away a long time ago — and honestly, I thought I had. But every time I sense that my season might be done, something inside whispers, not yet.

The Changing Why

When we first joined, Scouting was something I did for my kids — a way to give them what I had as a boy. Later, it became about leadership: building youth-led programs, watching young people surprise themselves.

Now, it's something deeper. It's about family — not just the one under my roof, but the one God built through this program.

When we moved to Florida, we didn't have family nearby. Scouting became that family. The campouts, committee meetings, and evenings around the fire filled the gap. There were people who cheered when things went right and showed up when they didn't. Families aren't perfect, but love isn't the absence of struggle — it's the choice to keep showing up anyway.

That's why I stay.

The Chief's Challenge

At the 2025 Scoutmasters Camporee, I chose the theme "Why We Scout." Each year there's a 5K run, but this time I wanted to turn it into something more — a personal challenge to every Scout and Scouter to push themselves a little farther. So I issued The Chief's Challenge, inviting anyone willing to run with the Chief.

I'd started distance running the previous summer at camp, trading my stationary bike for the open trail. What began as exercise soon became a habit of perseverance — a way to live the words "physically strong" and to encourage the Scouts in my care to do the same.

When the camporee came, I couldn't actually run — an injury sidelined me that weekend — but I still wanted others to have the experience. The medals were ready, glossy with the camporee logo on one side and a label on the back reading, "I Completed the Chief's Challenge." They weren't awards for speed, but reminders of effort and heart.

That weekend taught me something lasting: leadership isn't about being first across the finish line. Sometimes it's about cheering from the sidelines, celebrating others' progress, and knowing your role was to issue the invitation. The real win wasn't the miles run, but the confidence sparked in those who tried.

"I Wish I Could Do More"

I still think of Gary McKee's words. They used to sound like regret; now they sound like worship. A servant's heart always has one more mile to give, even when the trail seems done. That phrase has become my quiet prayer — not for more work, but for the strength to keep saying yes.

Why I Stay

I stay because of the youth who walk in shy and leave with confidence.

I stay because of the parents who nervously step up to help and discover their own "why."

I stay because I still see the boy from Jackson Avenue, the young Airman, the reluctant leader — in every Scout who learns to trust the process.

Brotherhood has carried me farther than any rank or title. In the Order of the Arrow, I found a family of quiet servants — people who live out cheerful service without seeking credit. That spirit taught me that leadership is shared, not owned; that every act of service links us into a greater circle of purpose.

Years ago, Simon Sinek's Start with Why reshaped how I led. We stopped chasing badges and started chasing purpose. When the "why" took root, everything else followed naturally — teamwork, advancement, even faith. The same question that transformed my troop keeps transforming me.

So when people ask why I still Scout, the truth is simple:
- Because this is how I serve.
- Because this is where I see God move.
- Because somewhere out there, a young person will need a leader who believes in them — just as others once believed in me.

And maybe, through that simple act of showing up, they'll find their own why.

Faith and Service as One Path

Scouting's ideals — shaped by the Scout Oath and Law — have become the cadence of my walk with God. Every commitment, every good turn, has been an echo of His greater call: to love and to lead through serving.

Every time I think the path might finally be leveling out, God turns it just enough to remind me there's still more to do, more to learn, more to give. That's okay. I don't need to see the whole trail to keep walking.

If I've learned anything, it's that our callings rarely come with clear directions — just a compass and a quiet voice that says, keep going.

And when that voice whispers again, I'll answer the same way I did at the start: Here am I. Send me.

CLOSING CAMPFIRE -
The Path I Didn't Expect

Looking back, I can see how every turn, every change, and every moment of uncertainty was part of God's design.

This wasn't the path I planned, but it was always the one I needed — the place where He met me in the ordinary and made it meaningful.

Through family, faith, and Scouting, I've learned that service is more than action; it's worship.

And though I still don't know every bend ahead, I trust the One who leads.

The path I didn't expect has become the journey I'm most grateful to walk — grateful for every mile already walked and every unseen step still ahead.

My Trail Companions
(Acknowledgments)

"I thank my God every time I remember you." — *Philippians 1:3*

This section is both a closing prayer and a word of thanks — to the people who walked beside me, believed in me, and helped me hear God's call more clearly. The path wasn't walked alone; it was built by the faithful steps of many who shared the trail.

1. Family

Mom and **Dad** – for modeling faith, perseverance, and quiet generosity long before I had the words to name them. Everything I've built stands on what you taught by living.

Amanda – for saying "yes" before I was ready, and for walking every unexpected mile with me.

William, Ben, and **Matthew** – for teaching me what it means to lead with love and to trust God's timing in every season.

Grandpa Anderson – for humor and grit that keep me grounded.

Grandpa Pinkley – for the workshop wisdom that built projects and character.

Their quiet strength and patience made space for obedience and growth.

2. Brothers in Scouting

Gary McKee – for showing that true service has no finish line.

Larry Hribar and **Herb Bradshaw** – the "Three Musketeers" of Buccaneer District; brothers in Scouting and laughter.

Matt Vercher – for opening the door and reminding me how connection builds community.

Frank Rivera – for reawakening my call to cheerful service and helping me find a home in the Order of the Arrow.

Kevin Creighton – for carrying the torch with quiet strength when it was time to pass it on.

Alex Christiansen – for reminding me that youth leadership is alive and well; your courage to lead lit a spark for others.

> *Leadership is never a solo act; every success was shared around a campfire of commitment and care.*

3. Church & Faith Family

Pastor Ryan Hall and the men of Wesley Church — for providing a place to rest, renew, and serve again.

Reverend Francie Dailey – for seeing youth as the heartbeat of the church and teaching me to listen for God's call early.

Pastor Bill – for blessing the start of our marriage and modeling calm, steadfast faith.

Tim Henson and **David Knarr** – lifelong friends whose laughter and loyalty marked the earliest chapters of my faith journey.

> *The church has always been more than a building; it's the people who walk with you when God calls you forward.*

4. Mentors & Teachers

Mr. Ewald, Mr. Brown, Mr. Smith, and **Mr. Plas** – for patience, creativity, and the freedom to explore how things work.

Billy Turk and **Woody Crist** – for teaching that obedience and trust go hand in hand, and that confidence grows from earned responsibility.

> *Every mentor taught something different — together, they built the foundation of faith and persistence.*

5. Fellow Servants

To everyone who volunteered, led, or followed faithfully — Scouts, Scouters, family, and friends.

To those who prayed quietly, offered advice, or reminded me to slow down.

To every runner who joined The Chief's Challenge and showed that leadership begins with showing up.

> *Service multiplies through example; I am only one of many hands doing His work.*

6. Gratitude & Hope

"Not to us, Lord, not to us, but to Your name be the glory." — *Psalm 115:1*

As I look back on this journey, my deepest gratitude is to God — for patience, redirection, and grace that never ran out.

The path I didn't expect continues still, and I pray these pages remind others that obedience is worth the risk, and service is never wasted.

Gratitude has become the quiet addition to my own Scout Law — a daily reminder that everything learned, shared, and lived along this path is grace undeserved but deeply appreciated.

Trail Map

The journey doesn't end at the last page. The Trail Map is here to help you keep walking — one honest look, one faithful step at a time.

In this section:

SEGMENT I -
The Quiet Call

"When the time is right, I, the Lord, will make it happen." — Isaiah 60:22

Before purpose is spoken aloud, it grows in small, ordinary spaces. This first stretch invites you to examine the quiet beginnings and unseen foundations that have carried you farther than you realized.

Trail Questions

1. Which early limits or losses ended up protecting something God was forming in you?
2. Where did you mistake God's preparation for His absence, and what do you see now that you couldn't then?
3. Whose unseen faithfulness built a floor you still stand on, and what specifically did they model?
4. What habits taught you to notice God's nudges (not just hear about them), and how will you guard those habits now?
5. What false starts or "nearlys" prepared you to recognize the real yes when it came?

Next Step: Write a brief note (or text) to one person whose quiet faith steadied you. Name the exact moment they helped.

Segment II -

Learning to Lead by Letting Go

"For even the Son of Man did not come to be served, but to serve." — Mark 10:45

Leadership sharpened when control got in the way. This section presses into humility, authority, and the courage to create space for others to rise.

Trail Questions

1. Where did your preference for order disguise a fear of failure, and what would trust look like there now?

2. Identify a standard you enforced that wasn't central to the mission. What deeper value were you trying to protect?

3. Whose growth stalled because you solved the problem for them? How could you re-enter now as a coach instead of a fixer?

4. What decision did you defend with policy that really needed patience, and what would patience have changed?

5. What would it require of you to step back intentionally so others can take greater ownership in your current setting?

Next Step: Choose one task you normally own. Hand it off with clear guardrails and a date to review outcomes — not performance.

SEGMENT III -
Listening to Leave

"Since we live by the Spirit, let us keep in step with the Spirit." — *Galatians 5:25*

Release is part of obedience. This stretch explores discernment, timing, and the grace to step aside without bitterness.

Trail Questions

1. Where are you most tempted to confuse momentum with calling?

2. List the costs of staying and the costs of going — then name which costs draw you closer to Christ-likeness.

3. What relational "cliques" or cultures made you feel out of step? What did that discomfort expose in you that needed refining?

4. When silence met your initiative, what did you learn about God's pace versus yours?

5. What would faithfulness look like if your contribution remains unseen or uncredited?

Next Step: Fast from one persuasive activity (emails, proposals, nudges) for a week and replace it with listening prayer for the people involved.

SEGMENT IV -
Rooted Again

> *"So then, just as you received Christ Jesus as Lord, continue to live in him, rooted and built up in him..."* — Colossians 2:6–7

Being replanted asks for patience — deep work beneath the surface before fruit returns. This stretch considers belonging, rebuilding, and stability without stagnation.

Trail Questions

1. Which old strengths don't transplant well to your new soil, and which must be pruned to grow?

2. What local practices (not just programs) prove you're committed to people over projects?

3. Where are you rebuilding faster than trust can carry, and what cadence would let roots take?

4. Who in your new context holds quiet authority you need to learn from — and what will you ask them first?

5. What boundary (time, scope, pace) will protect long obedience here?

Next Step: Walk your own ground this week — literally. Take a slow lap around your home, neighborhood, or work space and thank God for where He has planted you. Ask what faithfulness looks like right here, right now.

SEGMENT V -
The Path Ahead

"I press on toward the goal for the prize of the upward call of God in Christ Jesus."
— *Philippians 3:14*

Legacy isn't what bears your name; it's what outlives your presence. This final stretch turns toward stewardship, succession, and hope.

Trail Questions

1. If you left tomorrow, what would continue because it's owned by others — not you?

2. Name one conviction you will not compromise and one preference you're willing to release. Why each?

3. Where does your influence need to get smaller so others' responsibility can grow?

4. Who is your next "yes" — the specific person you will invest in without a title attached?

5. What blessing or benediction do the people you lead most need to hear from you this year?

Next Step: Write a two-sentence "hand off vision" a successor could use today. Share it with the person you're quietly preparing.

The Path Continues

The trail doesn't end here. Every lesson, every moment of surrender and service, becomes part of the next chapter God is writing through you.

You've walked through listening, letting go, rooting again, and pressing on — now it's time to walk with others.

Keep Walking

- Schedule two unhurried conversations this month — with a neighbor and a quiet servant in your church or team. Ask what healthy community, leadership, or pace looks like to them. Listen more than you speak.

- Choose one habit from this book to practice intentionally for thirty days — prayer, journaling, gratitude, or service — and note what changes as you do.

- Revisit your "small yeses." Which ones have grown into steady obedience? Which need to be renewed?

Remember: the path continues not because the work is unfinished, but because faith keeps moving.

Trail Log

These pages are here for you.

They're meant to help you pay attention to the moments that form your walk —
the steps, nudges, lessons, and small acts of faith that can be easy to miss in the
pace of life.

The Trail Log isn't a checklist or a report.
There's no right way to fill it out. Use it however it serves you best:

- Capture a moment that meant something.

- Record a lesson or nudge you don't want to forget.

- Note an act of service, gratitude, or a step of obedience.

- Track your journey through the Parts of the book — if you want to.

The pages that follow are rotated to give you more space for writing.

Turn the book sideways, take your time, and let these entries become a quiet
record of where God meets you on the trail.

Start anywhere you like.

Date	What God Showed Me	Action / Gratitude / Reflection

Date	What God Showed Me	Action / Gratitude / Reflection

Date	What God Showed Me	Action / Gratitude / Reflection

Your Trail Guide

About the Author

Guided by his faith in Christ, Allen Pinkley is a husband and Scoutmaster living with his wife, Amanda, on Florida's Space Coast. After years of quiet prompting to write, he finally said yes one Sunday morning when the pieces came together — and The Path I Didn't Expect began to take shape.

Through his service in Scouting and his volunteer work at Wesley UMC, Allen strives to make people feel seen and valued, trusting that Jesus meets us right where we are. When he isn't mentoring youth or serving at church, he enjoys caring for saltwater aquariums and spending time with Amanda — often walking through parks they enjoy together.

He hopes this story encourages others to listen when God stirs the heart and to trust that Christ is already at work in their path ahead.

Steady Current Press

Thoughtfully written stories that inspire growth, faith, and intentional living—encouraging reflection, purpose, and steady forward movement in everyday life.

Steady Current Press exists to publish work that forms character, deepens faith, and strengthens resolve in the ordinary rhythms of life. We believe meaningful change rarely arrives in dramatic moments. It grows through steady obedience, quiet courage, and daily intention.

We publish:

- Personal narratives of faithful service

- Reflections on spiritual formation

- Leadership rooted in humility and character

- Stories that move readers toward purposeful living

Writers whose work reflects these values are invited to connect at steadycurrentpress.com.

Love God —

— Love People

www.ingramcontent.com/pod-product-compliance
Lightning Source LLC
Chambersburg PA
CBHW051455130726
47987CB00005B/2332